CH

GET INTO CITIZEN SCIENCE

GET-INTO-IT GUIDES

VIC KOVACS

CRABTREE
Publishing Company
www.crabtreebooks.com

GET-INTO-IT GUIDES

Author: Vic Kovacs

Publishing plan research and development: Reagan Miller

Editors: Marcia Abramson, Petrice Custance

Photo research: Melissa McClellan

Editorial director: Kathy Middleton

Proofreader: Wendy Scavuzzo

Cover/interior design: T.J. Choleva

Production coordinator and prepress technician: Samara Parent

Print coordinator: Margaret Amy Salter

Consultant: Brianne Manning
Science teacher, Peel District School Board

Written and produced for Crabtree Publishing by BlueApple*Works* Inc.

Photographs

Shutterstock.com: © Nanette Grebe (cover center right); © VP Photo Studio (cover center bottom); © Menno Schaefer (cover center left); © Noradoa (cover top); cover clockwise from top right: © Al Mueller, © Paul Reeves Photography, © Lucky Business, © Vadim Sadovski, © Triff, © Africa Studio, © Melinda Fawver, see Austen Photography, © shipfactory, © paulista, © Matthew Clemente (TOC) © Jacek Chabraszewski (TOC bottom right); © Daniel Prudek (p. 6 left); © Miroslav Halama (p. 6 bottom right); © Tony Moran (p. 7 top left); © JuneJ (p. 7 top right); © Ger Bosma Photos (p. 7 middle left); © yhelfman (p. 7 bottom right); © espies (p. 10 left); © lanych (p. 10 right); © ZoomTravels (p. 11 top); © Henryk Sadura (p. 11 bottom); © Oleg Krugliak (p. 14 background); © Ryan M. Bolton (p. 15 top, top left); © Melinda Fawver (p. 15 top right); © Ilias Strachinis (p. 15 top middle); © Konrad Mostert (p. 15 bottom left); © Tom Reichner (p. 15 middle left); © Steve Byland (p. 15 middle bottom, 16 right); © Alexander Sviridov (p. 15 bottom right); © gregg williams (p. 16 top right); © Marina Zezelina (p. 15 top right background); © vagabond54 (p. 16 left); © Madlen (p. 17 top); © tantrik71 (p. 17 2cd from top); © MasterQ (p. 17 3rd from top); © FotoReques (p. 17 4th from top); © Sue Robinson (p. 17 bottom); © Vasilyev Alexandr (p. 17 bottom middle); © Vishnevskiy Vasily (p. 17 bottom 3rd from left); Eag1eEyes (p. 17 bottom left); © Melinda Fawver(p. 18 left); © SIMON SHIM (p. 18 right); © Kirsanov Valeriy Vladimirovich (p. 19 top); © yothinpi (p. 19 middle right); © tlindsayg (p. 19 bottom left); © Elliotte Rusty Harold (p. 20 bottom left); © Fer Gregory (p. 20 middle); © Peter Waters (p. 22 top, left, 25 middle left); © Glass and Nature (p. 22 right middle); © Elizaveta Kirina (p. 22 right); © emkaplin (p. 23 bottom right); Gitcevich Igor (p. 23 bottom right); lev radin (p. 23 top, 2cd from left); Leena Robinson (p. 23 top, 2cd from right); Julee75 (p. 23 top right); © Matee Nuserm (p. 23 top far right); © David Byron Keener/Shutterstock.com (p. 24 top); © Mark Baldwin (p. 24 bottom background); © Paul Reeves Photography (p. 25 middle); nienora (p. 26–27 background); © Martchan (p. 28 bottom left); © Peangdao (p. 28 bottom middle); © John D Sirlin (p. 28 bottom right); © FotoMonkey (p. 29 right).

© Sam Taylor: p. 4 left, 5 bottom, 8 bottom, 14, 21, 28 top right

© Austen Photography: p. 9, 12, 13 bottom, 19 right, 19 left, 24, 25, 27 top, 31

Creative Commons: Katja Schulz (p. 6 top right, 13 top left); Judy Gallagher (p. 20 top); Quit007 (p. 20–21 background); Bfpage (p. 23 top left); Hans Bernhard (Schnobby) (p. 26 top); European Southern Observatory (ESO) (p. 26 middle left);

Public Domain: NPS Photo by Kevin Bacher (TP, p. 4 right, 5 top, 8 top, 13 top right); Marc Imhoff/NASA GSFC, Christopher Elvidge/NOAA NGDC; Image: Craig Mayhew and Robert Simmon/NASA GSFC (p. 27 bottom right); US NOAA (p. 29 left); NASA image courtesy Jeff Schmaltz, MODIS Land Rapid Response Team at NASA GSFC (p. 29 middle)

Courtesy of Urban Buzz: p. 19 middle

Joshua Avramsom: p. 22 map based on Monarch Watch map

Courtesy of CosmoQuest: p. 26 right

Library and Archives Canada Cataloguing in Publication

Kovacs, Vic, author
        Get into citizen science / Vic Kovacs.

(Get-into-it guides)
Includes index.
Issued in print and electronic formats.
ISBN 978-0-7787-3636-3 (hardcover).--
ISBN 978-0-7787-3645-5 (softcover).--
ISBN 978-1-4271-1961-2 (HTML)

        1. Research--Citizen participation--Juvenile literature. 2. Science--Social aspects--Juvenile literature. 3. Research--Juvenile literature. I. Title.

Q180.55.C54K68 2017   j500   C2017-903612-2
                                                                      C2017-903613-0

Library of Congress Cataloging-in-Publication Data

CIP available at the Library of Congress

Crabtree Publishing Company
www.crabtreebooks.com   1-800-387-7650

Printed in Canada/092017/PB20170719

Published in Canada
Crabtree Publishing
616 Welland Ave.
St. Catharines, Ontario
L2M 5V6

Published in the United States
Crabtree Publishing
PMB 59051
350 Fifth Avenue, 59th Floor
New York, New York 10118

Published in the United Kingdom
Crabtree Publishing
Maritime House
Basin Road North, Hove
BN41 1WR

Published in Australia
Crabtree Publishing
3 Charles Street
Coburg North
VIC, 3058

CONTENTS

CITIZEN SCIENTISTS

Citizen science is a way for everyday people to collect data and share it with researchers who use it to gain a better understanding of the world. **Amateur** scientists have been contributing to different fields for centuries, but the term "citizen scientist" is still fairly new. Today's citizen science movement came about as a way to move science out of labs and back into the real world. Citizen science gets people to care about science by encouraging people to better understand the natural world—starting with the world right outside their window!

Some investigations require small groups. Others can be done alone.

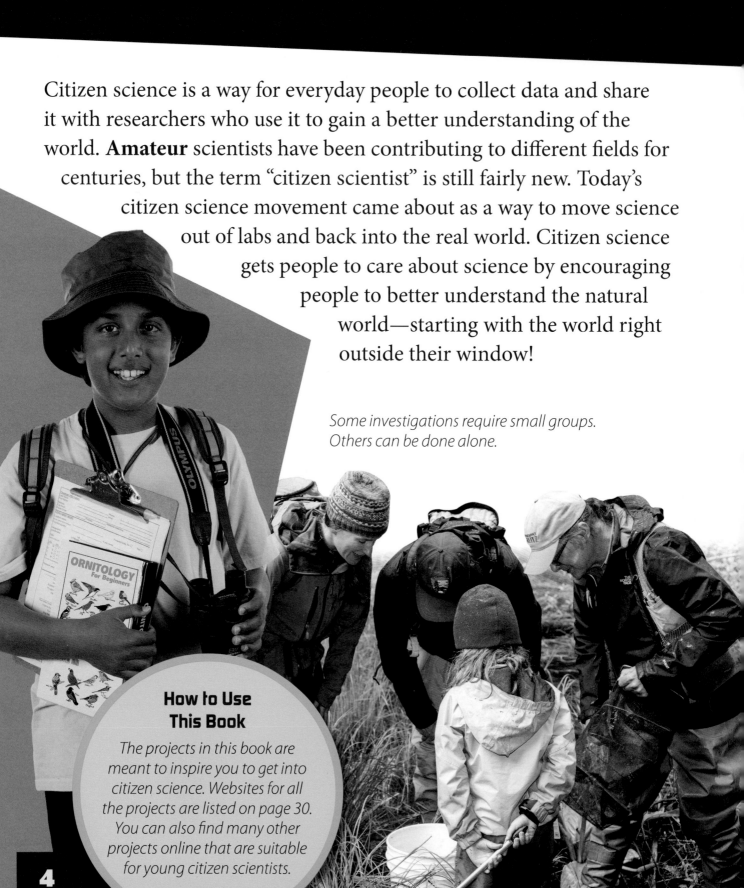

How to Use This Book

The projects in this book are meant to inspire you to get into citizen science. Websites for all the projects are listed on page 30. You can also find many other projects online that are suitable for young citizen scientists.

PROJECTS FOR EVERYONE

Part of the fun of citizen science is that anyone can get involved! No matter your age or where you live, you can be a citizen scientist. And no matter what part of the natural world you're interested in, you can find a project to get excited about! Just a few of the fields that use data collected by citizen

People of all ages volunteer together as citizen scientists.

scientists include ornithology (the study of birds), entomology (the study of insects), meteorology (the study of weather), and astronomy (the study of **celestial** objects such as planets and stars). There might be a project that's specifically about the area you live in, or one that's about a particular season. Some can even be done right in your own backyard, or at school! Whatever projects interest you the most, you can be sure that your contributions can help real scientists make important discoveries about the world.

ONLINE RESOURCES

There are a number of online resources for budding citizen scientists. One of the best is SciStarter. Most of the projects mentioned in this book can be found on SciStarter. The site also has a useful search function, so if you have a topic you're interested in, you can just type it in and see if there are any current projects related to it. Scientific American also has a great list of current projects that can be grouped by age level. The Citizen Science Center produces a newsletter with updates about new citizen science projects that you can subscribe to at its website.

Citizen science is a great way to learn about the world around you and help science move forward at the same time. Whatever you're interested in, there's a project out there right now with your name on it.

Today's technology makes collecting and sharing data easier.

CHANGING ECOSYSTEMS

Human beings have always had an effect on their environment. However, in the last 50 years, scientists have noted that these changes have been increasing. Human actions such as burning **fossil fuels** can affect **ecosystems** in dramatic ways. For example, rising temperatures are causing many species in North America to move their habitats farther north, or to higher areas, where it's cooler. The use of pesticides on farms and gardens can kill off species such as bees, which play an important role in helping plants reproduce.

Some citizen scientists help by sharing information at school and community events.

This is an area in which citizen scientists can be a huge help. These changes are so broad that it's impossible for any single group of scientists to track them. However, by enlisting the help of citizen scientists in every part of the world, they can gather data that they otherwise wouldn't have the resources to collect. Here are just a few things citizen scientists are helping researchers learn about today:

POLLINATORS

Pollinators are animals that spread **pollen** from one part of a plant to another, which makes the plant able to grow seeds. Without pollinators, plants cannot reproduce and spread. The most famous pollinators are bees, but other species such as ants, hummingbirds, and bats often perform the same function. Bee populations have recently been in decline. Citizen scientists are helping to track and count these populations to get a better understanding of their numbers.

FROGS AND WETLANDS

Wetlands, such as swamps and marshes, are important ecosystems. They perform many key functions, including purifying water, controlling flooding, and removing carbon dioxide from the air. One way scientists track how well wetlands are doing is through frog populations. If there are plenty of frogs, the ecosystem is healthy. However, if frog populations are low, or are noticeably decreasing, it might mean that the wetland is in trouble. Citizen scientists play an important role in helping to track these numbers.

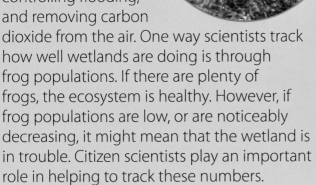

BIRD MIGRATIONS

Many species of birds do not live in the same place year-round. Starting in the fall, as the days turn cooler, these birds leave their breeding grounds in more northern parts of the world and fly south for the winter. Citizen scientists help by cataloging exactly when these species begin migrating, how large their flocks are, and if they're landing in places they weren't before. These efforts can help scientists figure out how changing ecosystems are affecting bird populations and their lifestyles.

INTRODUCED SPECIES

Sometimes, human beings introduce species into areas where they do not usually live. This was the case with the multicolored Asian ladybug (shown on the left), which was introduced into North America by the U.S. government in an attempt to control **aphid** populations. Some citizen science projects focus on how and where introduced species spread in their new area, and how their populations grow or decline.

WHERE DO THEY GO?

For decades, one of the greatest mysteries in natural science was "Where do monarch butterflies spend their winters?" Dr. Fred Urquhart of Canada was fascinated by this question. He and his wife, Norah, experimented with different ways to track the butterflies. However, they soon realized they would need help. This led to a call for volunteers to help track monarch **migration** routes, starting in 1952. Thousands of volunteers answered the call. By 1975, they helped discover the butterfly's winter habitat in Mexico. This was one of the earliest and most successful citizen science projects.

Along with tracking monarch butterflies, citizen volunteers are growing more milkweed for monarch caterpillars to eat.

RECORD, SKETCH, SHOOT— HAVE FUN!

The two most important skills a citizen scientist needs are the ability to observe and the ability to catalog. Many of the things citizen scientists are looking for are very small, or blend in easily with their surroundings, or both! However, there might be other clues that let you know the specimen you're looking for is close by. For example, birds and frogs often have very distinct sounds, or calls, that they make. These calls can help you identify a species, even if you can't see it.

Citizen scientists look high and low when they are observing the natural world.

CATALOGING YOUR DISCOVERIES

After you've observed the animal or **phenomena**, you're looking for, it's important to catalog it. This means keeping a record of exactly what you've seen or heard. These records are then submitted to scientists or institutions that use them to help draw conclusions. How you choose to catalog is completely up to you! You can use skills you already have, or you can use a citizen science project as a reason to develop new talents. Say you come across a bird you've been looking for. You could write a description of it, noting the colors of its feathers, its size, the shape of its beak, and what its call sounds like. Or, you could bring along a sketchbook and draw it lounging on a branch. You could also bring along a camera and practice your photography skills!

FIELD JOURNAL

Regardless of the area you're interested in, every citizen scientist needs one essential piece of equipment: a field journal! This is a notebook that you use to keep track of all your scientific observations. Any notebook could serve this function, but one with a hard cover is probably best. After all, in the field, you can't always find a flat surface to write on. Once you've got a field journal chosen, what do you put in it? For starters, every journal entry should include the date and time, the location, and the weather conditions.

Beyond basics like this, the most important thing to put in your field journal is your observations. If you're counting frogs, take notes on how many individual frogs you can hear, what species you can identify, and how often they're croaking. You can also make sketches of anything you see, or print out photos and paste them onto the journal pages for the day you took them. Just remember that it's YOUR journal, so feel free to personalize it however you like.

ENGAGE THE INATURALIST COMMUNITY

More than 400,000 people have signed up as citizen scientists with iNaturalist, an online network that aims to create "a living record of life on Earth."

When three college students in California came up with the idea for iNaturalist in 2008, they had no idea how popular it would become. By 2014, the site had more than a million observations and had become part of the California Institute of Sciences.

By mid-2017, iNaturalist has grown to more than five million observations contributing to 9,000 projects.

The website is easy to use with simple directions to follow. You can record observations directly or use a mobile app on your phone. Once you post an entry, check back to see what other citizen scientists have to say about it!

You can even get help with homework from the hundreds of nature guides posted by the site's users. And if you find a mystery organism, you can connect with experts to help you identify it.

TAKING GOOD PICTURES

Smartphone cameras are great to take close-up pictures of insects and small animals. Today's smartphone cameras can autofocus, zoom, have settings for different lighting conditions, and are very convenient to use. Smartphone cameras do have limitations, though. They are not as powerful as other types of cameras. If you're taking pictures of faraway birds or wildlife, a different kind of camera is needed, and experts recommend using one with a long zoom lens. This will not only allow for clearer images, but will also let you take photos from farther away. This lessens your chances of scaring animals away by getting too close.

HOLD STILL

When taking a photo, make sure nothing gets in front of the lens, which often happens with a smartphone. You can also block the flash by mistake. To keep the camera steady, stand with your legs very slightly apart and brace your body. Also, be sure to hold the camera with both hands—if you hold the camera in only one hand, pressing the button to take the photo will cause the camera to shake. Many cameras have image stabilization built into the camera or lens, but it is still important to hold the camera still.

PHOTO TIP

Remember that wildlife is wild. Never approach an animal in the wild—any wild animal will attack to protect itself or its young. It's important to respect animals and their habitat.

Hold a smartphone at the bottom to keep the lens free of fingers.

Hold a camera with one hand under the lens.

FOCUSING A CAMERA

Most cameras now have autofocus (AF) features. They use a computer and one or more sensors to find the right setting and adjust the focus. Some AF systems have a single sensor, while others have many. Most cameras offer photo modes such as animal, portrait, still life, and landscape. Animal mode helps to capture moving subjects. Portrait mode makes the subject stand out because it is the only thing in focus.

To take a photo like this using a camera, place the butterfly in the center of the frame. Press the shutter button halfway down and hold it. Then move the camera until the butterfly is where you want it. Finally, press the shutter button all the way down to take the photo. With a smartphone, you would tap on the butterfly on the screen to focus on it.

WHAT'S THE ANGLE?

When photographers take your class photos, they center the camera to capture everybody's smiling face the same way. But for other subjects, you can take a more interesting photo if you change your position. The viewpoint of a photo depends on the position of the camera. If the camera is below the subject, or above the subject, or to the side of the subject, it changes the viewpoint of the photo. Taking the photo from an unusual angle will capture and hold your viewer's attention.

GET IT RIGHT!

Good photos can make your observations of nature even better. You can find many photo tips on iNaturalist. Here are some basics:

Limit each photo to one type of animal, alone or in a group. The subject should fill about three-quarters of the frame, so you may need to zoom in.

Photograph marine animals and plants in the water so they look natural. If the subject is a plant, try to photograph its flowers and fruit as well as its leaves.

Whatever your subject, keep the focus sharp and the colors natural. Avoid glare and shadows. Take images showing different features of the plant or animal and its environment.

Burst mode (or continuous shooting) is a great choice when you're taking photographs of a moving subject. You will have a lot of shots to delete, but you may end up with the perfect shot!

ECOSYSTEM EXPLORERS

BioBlitz

A BioBlitz is a group effort to document all the living plant and animal species that can be found in one place at one time—often in a single day or weekend. American naturalist, Susan Rudy, came up with the name while helping with the first-ever BioBlitz in 1996 in a park in Washington, D.C. The idea caught on fast because BioBlitzes, which often include food, music, and games, are as much fun as they are useful. Above all, they give citizen scientists and professional scientists an opportunity to team up and create a snapshot of **biodiversity**.

PROJECT:
BACKYARD BIOBLITZ

BioBlitzes are not formal research studies, so it's easy to host one. The location can be as large as Yellowstone National Park or as small as your own backyard. The organizers decide exactly what, when, and how to explore. You can run your own BioBlitz with your family and friends! With a bit of planning and a few supplies, you can learn a lot about nature just outside your door. Just follow these steps:

1. *Choose an area: Decide where you want to have your BioBlitz. Your own backyard? Your schoolyard? A park near your house? Make sure it's an area with clear boundaries so you don't get overwhelmed.*

2. *Set a time limit: How long do you want your BioBlitz to last? Half an hour to an hour is probably a good length for your first one.*

3. *Gather your supplies: Field guides are books that list different plant and animal species, usually with pictures for easy identification. There are also smartphone apps that can help, but make sure you ask your parents before downloading anything. As well as identification tools, you might want a camera to help you keep track. You'll definitely need a clipboard with some paper, and something to write with.*

RESULTS AREA

Every BioBlitz needs a place where people can display samples and record what they found. This could be a classroom at school or a corner of your porch or garage. Be sure to have an adult check out anything you find before you touch it. If there is any doubt about safety, just take a photo! Once the results are in, they can be posted by nature groups, universities, government agencies, or sites such as iNaturalist. Scientists use BioBlitzes as a starting point for more biodiversity studies.

WHAT IS A BIOLOGICAL RECORD?

A biological record shows where members of a particular species were found on a given date. An easy way to make a biological record is to think of the four W's: what, where, when, and who.

What: Start by naming the species. If possible, list both the common and scientific names. If you are not sure about the name, use iNaturalist or another source to get some help.
Where: Record exactly where you made the observation.
When: Be specific about the time, day, and date of the observation.
Who: It's important to include the name of the person who made the observation, in case there are questions later.

Did You Know?

A BioBlitz in Toronto, Canada, in 2014, discovered two species of spiders that were new to the country.

4   Get looking: Once all your preparations are done, get out there! Look anywhere you think bugs and animals might be hiding. Under rocks, in bushes, and on trees are all good places to start. Also take note of what kind of plant life is present. Once you identify something, make a note of it, and see how many others you can find!

5   Consider your findings: Gather together and count up how many different species you found, and how many individuals in each species. Then write the event report. You could also draw a map of where exactly you found everything.

6   Do it again: Try waiting a few months, or until the seasons change, then do another BioBlitz. Then you can compare your findings to see how the ecosystem changes over time, and with the seasons.

COUNTING FROGS

Frogs are amphibians, which are animals that live partly in water and partly on land. Frogs are sensitive to environmental changes in both these areas, such as the effects of pollution. This means scientists can learn a lot about the environmental health of an area based on its frog population. To help with this research, many citizen science projects have sprung up to monitor local frog populations. There are a few tips that can help you become an expert frog counter. Number one, frogs are often easier to hear than to see. Familiarizing yourself with frog calls in your area is a great place to start. Number two, frogs call most often at dusk, so that's usually the best time to listen. Also, frogs call most often during their breeding season, which is usually in the spring. Find out when the breeding season usually happens in your area. Lastly, it's easier to hear frogs on a still night, so try choosing an evening with little to no wind.

PROJECT: FROGWATCH USA

FrogWatch USA is a citizen science program that uses volunteers to monitor frogs in their area. The group has local chapters all over the country where volunteers can get training to learn about frogs in their community and how to submit their findings. An average evening of frog watching for a volunteer might go something like this:

When you listen for frogs, try closing your eyes. Some studies have found that this helps people concentrate.

1 *Find a good location: If you live near a lake or a pond, this might be as close as your back porch. If not, you might have to go a little bit farther. Make sure you stay safe, and have a parent accompany you.*

2 *Listen: It is recommended that you listen for at least three minutes at a time, but if you can listen for longer, great! You might want to bring along a recording device to help identify specific species later.*

3 *Record: Keep track of the number of frogs you can observe, and how often they're making calls. One night you might not see or hear any, and another you might hear several different individuals.*

4 *Submit: Once you get home, submit your findings to FrogWatch USA.*

Recognizing Frog Sounds

Not all frogs say "ribbit" like the ones in cartoons. Every species of frog has its own call. People most often hear the loud call of the males, who use a small sac in their throat to vibrate air and produce sound. That sound may be a peep, croak, click, chirp, or even a bark.

With so many different calls, it takes a lot of practice to tell frog and toad species apart by sound. You can start by listening to different calls on a nature website, or you can get an audio book from your local library or bookstore. Here are some sample calls to start you off:

Fowler's toad: "Waah" like a baby.

American toad: A wobbly musical sound that lasts up to 12 seconds.

American bullfrog: A loud, low-pitched drone or bellow.

Gray tree frog: A short and wobbly musical sound.

Green frog: A banjo-like twang.

Wood frog: A duck-like quack.

Northern leopard frog: A low, rattling snore.

Whale Migrations

On both the east and west coasts of North America, some citizen scientists have devoted themselves to tracking the migration patterns of whales. Their efforts help scientists to identify individual whales, which can teach them about the life cycle of these amazing animals. They also help to compile population numbers, which aids local governments in their **conservation** efforts.

COUNTING BIRDS

Most birds fly, which allows them to soar through the sky and visit many different places—but makes it hard for scientists to track and study. That's why citizen-science projects are so important in ornithology, or the study of birds. Each year, thousands of people help scientists determine how bird populations are changing and whether they are being affected by **climate change**, pollution, habitat loss, and disease. Ornithology projects may be local, continent-wide like Project FeederWatch, or even worldwide like the Great Backyard Bird Count.

PROJECT FEEDERWATCH

Project FeederWatch got its start in Canada more than 40 years ago. It is now a joint project of the Cornell University Lab of Ornithology in the state of New York and Bird Studies Canada. More than 20,000 people of all ages in almost every state and province participate. Volunteers experience both the fun of watching birds and the satisfaction of being part of an important scientific project. Many kids join in on their own, with their family, or as a school project.

Robins are considered a sign of spring, but they don't all go south for the winter. If there is food around, they may stay in one place.

Dove Expansion

*Volunteers helped scientists track the amazing spread of the Eurasian collared dove. This bird extended its **range** from the Middle East to Europe, then was brought to the Bahamas accidentally in 1974. By the 1990s, it was tracked in Florida. Now it is common all over North America, except in northeast states and provinces.*

THE MOST FREQUENT VISITOR

The dark-eyed junco really gets around. More than 80 percent of FeederWatchers report seeing this little sparrow, which has 12 regional forms with variations in color and markings.

PROJECT: GREAT BACKYARD BIRD COUNT

The Great Backyard Bird Count started in 1998, and is believed to be the first online citizen science project to study wild birds. It's another project of the Cornell Lab of Ornithology and Bird Studies Canada, along with the Audubon Society and Wild Birds Unlimited. People all over the world count birds during four days in February. More than 160,000 people now participate each year. They provide the data that enables scientists to put together a detailed picture of world bird populations.

Tip

Sunflower seeds attract the widest variety of birds. They especially like the black oil sunflower seeds rather than the big striped ones. Black oil seeds have thin shells that crack easily, and a high fat content to give birds energy.

SETTING UP A BIRD FEEDING STATION

Birds have adapted to a variety of foods. Some eat on the ground, while others feed in trees or even hover in the air! Learn what birds are common in your area and how they like to eat, then try a variety of feeders in your yard.

Tree Trunk Feeders

A cage-like feeder containing suet will attract woodpeckers, jays, wrens, and other birds that cling to trees.

Ground Level Feeders

Robins, mourning doves, sparrows, and grackles will come to a bird feeder raised just above the ground.

Platform Feeders

Cardinals, doves, and starlings like to feed on a raised platform on a windowsill, railing, or post.

Hanging Feeders

Hang up a tube feeder with small openings for finches and chickadees.

WATER SUPPLY

Even more than food, water will bring birds to your backyard. They especially need help with water during dry spells and during the winter, when they really appreciate a heated backyard birdbath.

INSECT INVESTIGATIONS

BUG WATCH

There are 1.5 million different insect species. All together, insects make up more than half of all the known animals on Earth! With such a huge variety of insects, it's not surprising that they carry out a number of different functions in nature. Some, such as bees, help to pollinate plants. Others, such as dung beetles, feed on the waste products of other animals and help to clean up their environments.

PROJECT: BUGS IN OUR BACKYARD

Bugs In Our Backyard is a citizen science project that allows citizen scientists of all ages to assist researchers simply by walking into their own backyards, looking for bugs, and noting what they find.

Through these surveys, researchers hope to learn about how and where different species are distributed, how populations are growing or shrinking, and how different species interact with each other and with their environments. Data submitted by citizen scientists becomes part of a publicly available database that can help to provide answers to these questions.

*If possible, take a look at the bugs you catch with a **loupe** or microscope. Some bugs look like creatures from a science fiction movie!*

INVADING STINKBUGS

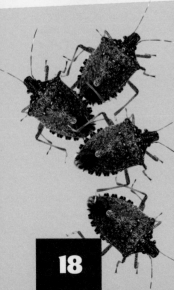

Stinkbugs are bugs that actually stink! They are just fine if you leave them alone. But if disturbed, they will emit a strong, unpleasant smell to ward off predators...and people. The brown marmorated stinkbug is a species of insect that isn't native to North America. It was first observed on the continent in 1998, in Allentown, Pennsylvania. Since then, it has spread to other parts of the country. As an invasive species, it has caused a number of problems. The largest problem is its tendency to damage crops. The website stinkbug-info.org allows citizen scientists to report areas where stinkbugs are present and how many there are. This helps scientists determine how and where they're spreading.

PROJECT: URBAN BUZZ

Cicadas are ancient insects that are helping modern scientists track climate change in a project called Urban Buzz. You can help, too, by sending them dead bugs!

Cicadas have a fascinating lifecycle. Adults lay eggs in tree branches. Once these eggs hatch, the babies, called nymphs, fall onto the ground and burrow into it. This is where cicadas spend the majority of their lives, with some species living underground for up to 17 years! Eventually, they emerge and shed their shells, becoming adults. Once fully grown, they live for up to six weeks. Most of their adult lives are spent breeding the next generation. Cicadas are also famous for the loud, droning buzz they make, which is mostly used as a mating call.

Did You Know?

The name cicada comes from the Latin word for "tree cricket." In China, many people like to snack on spicy fried cicadas!

Cicadas are sensitive to environmental factors including the spread of cities, climate change, and pollution. These may cause abnormal development of their legs and wings, and that is what Urban Buzz is studying. To help with the project, follow the simple steps below:

Collect Cicadas:

Locate and collect two to five cicadas. They can be alive or dead, but either way, make sure you freeze them when you get home.

Record Data:

*Urban Buzz has printable data sheets where you can record data such as GPS **coordinates** of where you found the cicada, the temperature when you found it, the cicada's sex, and the habitat in which it was found. Fill out one sheet per cicada.*

Send Them In:

Carefully pack the dead cicadas and your data sheets and send them through the mail to the Urban Buzz project. The mailing address can be found on the Urban Buzz website.

FIREFLY WATCH

Fireflies, despite their name, are actually winged beetles. Also called lightning bugs, there are around 2,000 species all over the world. They're famous for their ability to create light with special organs. This is known as bioluminescence, and is achieved by combining chemicals within the insect's own body. These lights serve a number of different purposes, with the most important being attracting mates. Recently, scientists have noticed that in many places, firefly populations are on the decline as humans move closer to traditional firefly habitats and disrupt natural light patterns.

Did You Know?

The light produced by fireflies is very efficient. All the energy that goes into creating it is given off as light. This is unlike most processes that create light, most of which also create heat. Because of this, the light emitted by fireflies is known as cold light.

1. **Choose your location:** If you have a yard, you're set. If not, try a field or marsh. Fireflies like warm, wet places.

2. **Register:** Go to the Firefly Watch website and sign up. You'll provide a description of the area you'll be watching, then you're good to go.

3. **Start observing:** Head to your study site and take note of how many fireflies you see. Even if you don't see any, make a note of that. The Firefly Watch website has a helpful form that you can print out to help you keep track of your data.

PROJECT: FIREFLY WATCH

Declining firefly populations led scientists at the Museum of Science in Boston to create the Firefly Watch program. Through this program, citizen scientists can help researchers shed light on these unique insects and the issues they face. Participating is fun, easy, and takes very little time. If you want to help, just follow the simple steps below, beginning on page 20:

4 *Report your observations: Log back onto the Firefly Watch site and fill out the observations form.*

GO FIGURE!

Flashing fireflies are hard to find in the western United States. Scientists don't know why, but there are fewer species of fireflies west of Kansas, and they glow only faintly or not at all!

POLLINATORS IN TROUBLE

Fireflies aren't the only insects with declining populations. Bee numbers have also been decreasing dramatically. This is a problem because of the role bees play as pollinators. Bees help plants reproduce, so a decline in their population can cause a decline in the success of many crops. This can have far-reaching effects for human beings. For example, without bees, farmers would have a harder time producing their crops, which would create serious food shortages. As a result, a number of projects have sprung up to document bee populations. These include Bee Hunt and Bumblebee Watch. With these projects, citizen scientists can help document the size and **distribution** of bee populations. This will help scientists not only understand how and why bee populations are in decline, but also what can be done to help them. If you choose to get involved in a bee watching project, it's important to remember that bees can be dangerous. If you want to start documenting bees, always have a parent or adult supervisor with you.

AMAZING MONARCH BUTTERFLIES

Monarchs, with their **distinctive** orange and black patterned wings, may be the most famous butterfly species. Like bees, they are an important pollinator species. Monarchs are famous for the incredible migration they make every year. Unlike many other insects, they cannot survive the winter, so they must fly south.

Monarchs that make their home west of the Rocky Mountains usually spend winter hibernating on the southern coast of California. Most Eastern monarchs fly all the way to Mexico—a journey that can span up to 3,000 miles (4,830 km). In the spring, they begin the long trip home. They stop to breed along the way and it may take three of four generations to finish the trip.

WINTERING IN MEXICO

Most of the monarchs from eastern North America winter each year at the Monarch Butterfly Biosphere Reserve in Mexico. The habitat, about 62 miles (100 km) northwest of Mexico City, is located in a rugged mountain forest. It was discovered in 1975 and has been named a United Nations World Heritage Site. In the fall, the habitat's pine and fir trees seem to turn orange as the monarchs cluster together for warmth. People come from all over the world to see them.

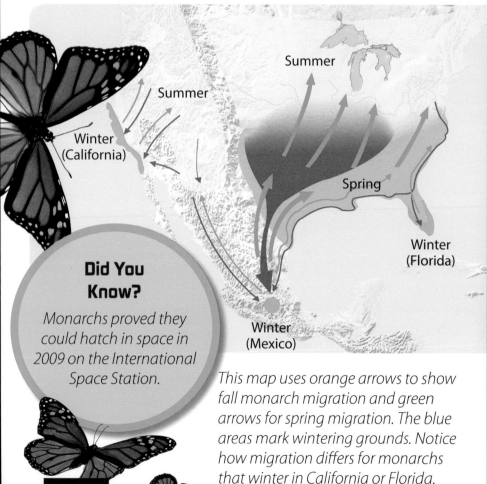

Summer

Summer

Winter
(California)

Spring

Winter
(Florida)

Winter
(Mexico)

Did You Know?

Monarchs proved they could hatch in space in 2009 on the International Space Station.

This map uses orange arrows to show fall monarch migration and green arrows for spring migration. The blue areas mark wintering grounds. Notice how migration differs for monarchs that winter in California or Florida.

A monarch's lifecycle is made up of four different stages. They start out as eggs, which hatch into caterpillars. This is known as their larval stage. After two weeks of eating their favorite food, milkweed plants, the caterpillars spin a cocoon called a chrysalis. This is their pupal stage, and it lasts for about ten days. Finally, a beautiful butterfly emerges and lives for four or five weeks.

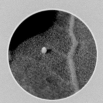
Monarch egg

Monarch caterpillar

Monarch chrysalis

Emerging monarch

Project: Monarch Watch

Monarch Watch started in 1991 at the University of Kansas. Every year, thousands of citizen scientists get involved with Monarch Watch and similar programs. Along with tracking monarchs, they often grow milkweed plants to help make up for the loss of habitat. Some raise monarchs at home or in the classroom, then release them into the wild. It's all an important effort because the number of monarchs keeps declining in North America. One of the projects involves catching and tagging butterflies to learn about their migration patterns!

How does monarch tagging work?

Each tag has a unique combination of three numbers and three letters that are coded to indicate the year of capture. The tags also tell how to contact Monarch Watch. Usually, tags are found after a monarch dies. By comparing where the butterfly was tagged and where it ended up, scientists learn about the migration and health of the species.

DRAGONFLY MIGRATION MONITORING

Monarch butterflies aren't the only migrating insects scientists are interested in. The Migratory Dragonfly Partnership is a collaboration that is trying to learn more about dragonfly migration. It has two main citizen science projects. The first, Pond Watch, involves regularly returning to the same pond or wetland and making notes on the numbers and types of dragonflies there, as well as their behavior. The second project, Migration Monitoring, specifically focuses on when and where dragonflies are migrating to and from, as well as behaviors such as mating. Dragonfly migration is still something of a mystery to researchers, and these projects can help to shed light on it. Information provided by citizen scientists also helps to ensure that migration routes are protected.

MONARCH TAGGING SKILLS

Catching and tagging monarch butterflies might seem difficult at first, but if you follow some simple steps, it's not actually too hard. First things first, you'll need some basic equipment. A butterfly net is probably the most important piece of equipment. You'll also want paper for writing down your finds, a clipboard to write on, and a pen or pencil to write with. And if you're tagging, you'll obviously need tags. You can buy a kit from the Monarch Watch website that comes with tags and data sheets that you can send back to the project. Before you head out, make sure you wash your hands so you don't get anything on the wings of any butterflies you catch.

TAG@KU.EDU
MONARCH WATCH
1-888-TAGGING
XXX 111

Butterflies are set free after tagging. It does not harm them and provides important data for scientists.

Migration season is the best time for tagging, so find out when monarchs usually leave or pass through your area. Fall is the most popular season for tagging, and late morning to afternoon is usually the best time. Once you've got your equipment ready, follow these steps:

1 *Find a location: Monarchs are pollinators, so anywhere with flowers is a good place to start. Your backyard, a stream, and riverbanks are all good places to look.*

2 *Find a butterfly: Butterflies can be hard to catch while they're in flight. Your best bet to snag one is to find one while it's feeding from a flower, or resting on a bush or a tree. Approach it carefully, so you don't scare it away.*

3 Catch a monarch: Once you are close enough, gently bring your net down over the butterfly. You want it to be near the back of your net so it can't fly away. Make sure your net is made of a soft mesh that won't harm the butterflies.

4 Prepare for tagging: Find a level spot so you are stable. Kneel down. Use your thumb and forefinger to grab all four of the butterfly's wings as shown above through the net.

5 Pick up the butterfly: Slide your free hand into the net. Now take hold of the butterfly with the hand inside the net, and let go with the hand outside the net. Slowly pull out the hand holding the butterfly. Hooks on its legs may catch on the net, so be very careful as you do this.

Mitten-shaped distal cell

Black scent glands on male monarch

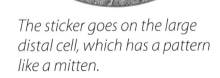

To find out a monarch's sex, look for a black spot in the middle of each hind wing. This is a scent gland which males use to attract a mate. Females don't have them.

The sticker goes on the large distal cell, which has a pattern like a mitten.

6 Keep a record: After you remove the butterfly from the net, note the sex and other information about the butterfly on your data sheet.

7 Place the tag: Locate the distal cell on the outside of the wing. Remove the tag from its sheet with your other hand and gently but firmly place it over the cell. This location makes sure the butterfly can still fly with the tag on.

8 Release the butterfly: Allow it to continue on its journey. After the migration season, don't forget to send in your data sheets!

YOUNG STARGAZERS

Astronomy is the study of celestial bodies such as planets, stars, and comets. It is possibly the oldest natural science, and has a long history of amateur astronomers who have helped to make important discoveries. In fact, one of the discoverers of the famous comet Hale-Bopp was an amateur astronomer. Today, there are a variety of projects that citizen scientists interested in astronomy can take part in. Here are just a few.

Hale-Bopp was named for the two Americans who found it in 1975: astronomer Alan Hale and citizen scientist Thomas Bopp.

PROJECT: COMET HUNTERS

There's more than just stars in the night sky! Main-belt comets are a newly discovered type of celestial object. They occur in our solar system's **asteroid belt**, but have tails that are usually associated with comets. Only about 10 are known today, but scientists are trying to find more. The Comet Hunters project was started as a way to **mobilize** citizen scientists to help with the search! By getting a larger number of people looking, the chance of finding more of these objects increases. The more that are found, the more researchers can learn not only about asteroid activity, but also about the origins of the universe! Volunteers help by combing through images of asteroids on the Comet Hunters website. If they discover any with a distinctive comet tail, they report it, and scientists check out the object with telescopes. This means that citizen scientists have a real chance at discovering a new, rare main belt comet!

A 1996 image shows 7968 Elst-Pizarro, the first known main-belt comet.

PROJECT: COSMOQUEST

CosmoQuest is a project that has **NASA** as a partner. It aims to help map out the surface of celestial objects. Projects include mapping out the surface of the moon, planets such as Mars and Mercury, and the giant asteroid Vesta. Citizen scientists help with these projects by examining images provided by NASA. They count surface features such as craters, and take note of their different sizes. By using large groups of citizen volunteers, scientists are able to learn about these bodies much more quickly.

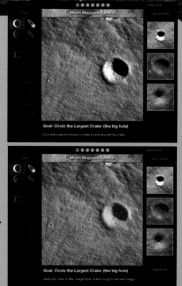

The CosmoQuest website provides tutorial sessions where you can learn how to map the Moon and planets properly.

PROJECT: GLOBE AT NIGHT

Globe at Night is a project that aims to raise people's awareness about the issues created by light pollution, and provide global mapping data for light pollution. Light pollution can lead to a number of problems, but one of the most obvious is that today, in most cities, it's nearly impossible to actually see stars in the night sky. The project asks citizen scientists to go outside on dark moonless nights and report how many stars are visible in particular **constellations**. Volunteers follow a few simple steps:

❶ *Go outside: Wait an hour after sunset but go before 10 p.m. You'll be heading out at night, so you'll need adult supervision. Go to a place such as a field or park where there are no lights directly above or around you. Once you're there, give your eyes a few minutes to adjust to the darkness.*

❷ *Locate your constellation: The Globe at Night website focuses on a different constellation every few months. They run 10-day observation campaigns every month. Check to see what the current constellation campaign is, and when it's running. The site will also provide you with resources to locate the constellation from your area. Once you're outside and your eyes have adjusted, look up and locate your constellation in the sky.*

❸ *Report: Globe at Night also has an app that can be accessed from a smartphone, tablet, or computer. Log on, and it will ask you a number of questions. These include where you're observing from, the time and date, how bright the stars are, and how much cloud cover is present. Once you've answered these questions, simply submit your report!*

You can observe for just one night, or you can observe multiple nights in a row. If you choose to do multiple nights, try observing from different locations to see how stargazing might differ from place to place!

LIGHT POLLUTION

Light pollution occurs when too much artificial light exists in an environment. It can come from things such as street lamps, billboard lights, or skyscrapers that leave their lights on. It can have serious effects on the environment. Not only is the night sky getting harder to see, but light pollution can also affect ecosystems. Some animals can become confused by artificial light, and sea turtle hatchlings have had difficulty getting to the ocean because streetlights **disorient** them. It's important to be aware of light pollution and do what you can to lessen it. This might be as simple as making sure you turn off all the lights in your house before bed. Every bit of effort helps.

Light pollution can be seen in highly populated areas in this image of Earth from NASA.

WEATHER WATCHERS

Most people don't think about the weather beyond wondering if they need to bring an umbrella with them when they leave the house. However, weather has a major effect on many aspects of our lives. If you're interested in learning more about the weather, from how it functions to how it affects humans, animals, and their ecosystems, these projects are worth checking out!

PROJECT: NASA GLOBE OBSERVER: CLOUDS

NASA GLOBE Observer: Clouds is a project in which citizen scientists assist NASA by observing clouds. These observations can help scientists learn about the planet's climate. Volunteer data is also used to make sure NASA satellites are functioning properly. Helping out is simple. All you need to do is download the Cloud Observer app, head outside, and start taking pictures of clouds! Follow the prompts to record your observations from below, and compare them with satellite images from above. It's a great way to learn, and to provide valuable help to scientists at the same time.

Like most of today's citizen science projects, NASA GLOBE has a smartphone app.

TYPES OF CLOUDS

Cloud names come from Latin words that describe their shape and height in the sky.

High Clouds

Wispy cirrus clouds are made of ice crystals.

Mid Clouds

Altocumulus is the most common mid cloud formation.

Low Clouds

Cumulonimbus are thunderstorm clouds that produce hail and tornadoes.

PROJECT: THE COMMUNITY COLLABORATIVE RAIN, HAIL, & SNOW NETWORK

The Community Collaborative Rain, Hail, & Snow Network, or CoCoRaHS, is a volunteer network that measures and tracks precipitation such as rain, hail, and snow. Whenever a storm travels through a volunteer's area, they measure how much precipitation fell, and use the CoCoRaHS website to report it. This helps to create a complete and accurate map of weather conditions across the country. This information is then used by the National Weather Service, state and local officials, and utility company managers.

PROJECT: CYCLONE CENTER

Cyclone Center is a citizen science project that studies tropical cyclones. A lot is still unknown about these dangerous storms. One of the main mysteries is exactly how fast winds blow inside a cyclone. Scientists believe the answers might lie in satellite photos. The project has more than 300,000 **infrared** satellite images that can be classified with something called the Dvorak Technique. However, there are far too many images for a single person to go through, and computers aren't as effective as humans at classifying them. That's where citizen scientists come in. By answering a few questions, they can help to build a database that can help predict the strength of future cyclones.

COUNTING PENGUINS IN ANTARCTICA

Although citizen science is more popular than ever, there are still some places where it's impossible. Antarctica is one of the coldest and hardest-to-reach areas of the planet. However, people have found a way around the continent's **inhospitable** weather. Penguin Watch is a group that uses cameras to observe penguin families. They supply classrooms with images from their cameras, and students are able to track changes in groups of penguins from November to January. Citizen science really is a global activity!

Satellite photos show the huge size of Hurricane Katrina, which devastated areas from Florida to Texas in 2005.

Hurricane, cyclone, and typhoon are all names for a rapidly rotating tropical storm. An English explorer created the name "cyclone" from a Greek word for "spin." In parts of Asia, the storms are called typhoons, a name that likely has Arabic roots. In the Americas, "hurricane" comes from the Spanish "huracán," which likely comes from the Mayan "hurikan."

LEARNING MORE

Books

Citizen Scientists: Be a Part of Scientific Discovery from Your Own Backyard by Loree Griffin Burns, Square Fish, 2012.

Ultimate Explorer Field Guide: Insects by Libby Romero, National Geographic Children's Books, 2017.

The Young Birder's Guide to Birds of North America by Bill Thompson III, Houghton Mifflin Harcourt, 2012.

Websites

iNaturalist
www.inaturalist.org

SciStarter
https://scistarter.com/

Scientific American
www.scientificamerican.com/citizen-science/

Citizen Science Center
www.citizensciencecenter.com/

Backyard Bioblitz
www.nationalgeographic.org/activity/backyard-bioblitz/

FrogWatch USA
www.aza.org/frogwatch

Project FeederWatch
http://feederwatch.org

Great Backyard Bird Count
http://gbbc.birdcount.org

Bugs In Our Backyard
www.bugsinourbackyard.org

Urban Buzz
http://studentsdiscover.org/lesson/urban-buzz-citizen-science-with-cicadas/

Firefly Watch
https://legacy.mos.org/fireflywatch/

Bee Hunt
www.discoverlife.org/bee/

Bumble Bee Watch
www.bumblebeewatch.org

Monarch Watch
http://monarchwatch.org

Dragonfly Pond Watch
http://pondwatch.org/index/welcome

Dragonfly Migration Monitoring Project
www.migratorydragonflypartnership.org/index/welcome

Comet Hunters
www.zooniverse.org/projects/mschwamb/comet-hunters

CosmoQuest
https://sandbox.cosmoquest.org/x/

Globe at Night
www.globeatnight.org

NASA GLOBE Observer: Clouds
https://scistarter.com/project/16830-NASA-GLOBE-Observer%3A-Clouds

The Community Collaborative Rain, Hail, and Snow Network
www.cocorahs.org

Cyclone Center
www.cyclonecenter.org

Penguin Watch
www.penguinwatch.org

GLOSSARY

amateur A person who does something (such as a sport or hobby) for pleasure but not as a job

aphid A small, soft-bodied insect that feeds by sucking juice from plants

asteroid belt The area between the orbits of Mars and Jupiter, which contains thousands of small planet-like bodies called asteroids

biodiversity The existence of a variety of plants and animals in an environment

celestial In the sky ot space, or relating to it

climate change Changes in Earth's weather patterns

conservation The protection of animals, plants, and natural resources

constellation A group of stars that forms a particular shape in the sky

coordinates Numbers that are used to locate a point on a map, such as longitude and latitude

disorient To make a person or animal lost or confused

distinctive Having a special or unusual quality

distribution How numbers of a plant or animal are spread out over an area

ecosystem All the living things in an area and how they interact with each other and with their environment

fossil fuel A fuel (such as coal, oil, or natural gas) that is formed in the earth from dead plants or animals

infrared Invisible light at the red end of the spectrum

inhospitable Unwelcoming; hard to survive in

loupe A small magnifier that may be attached to eyeglasses or hand-held

migration The act of moving from one place to another on a regular basis

mobilize To gather and make ready for action

NASA The National Aeronautics and Space Administration of the United States, also known as the space agency

phenomena Remarkable occurrences

pollen A fine powder, usually yellow, that is made by some plants so they can reproduce

range The geographical area in which an organism can be found living

INDEX